Time Management

90 Minute Guides

Michelle N. Halsey

ISBN-10: 1-64004-038-2
ISBN-13: 978-1-64004-038-0

Contents

Chapter 1 – Setting SMART Goals

Time management training most often begins with setting goals. These goals are recorded and may be broken down into a project, an action plan, or a simple task list. Activities are then rated based on urgency and importance, priorities assigned, and deadlines set. This process results in a plan with a task list or calendar of activities. Routine and recurring tasks are often given less focus to free time to work on tasks that contribute to important goals.

This entire process is supported by a skill set that should include personal motivation, delegation skills, organization tools, and crisis management. We'll cover all this and more during this workshop.

At the end of this tutorial, you should be able to:

- Plan and prioritize each day's activities in a more efficient, productive manner

- Overcome procrastination quickly and easily

- Handle crises effectively and quickly

- Organize your workspace and workflow to make better use of time

- Delegate more efficiently

- Use rituals to make your life run smoother

- Plan meetings more appropriately and effectively

Encourage participants to write their own workshop objectives in their guide.

Before reviewing this chapter, answer the following questions:

- What are your biggest time wasters?

- What are you currently doing to manage your time?

- What could you be doing better?

- If you came away from this workshop with only one thing, what would that be?

Take a moment to discuss these questions and note answers on the flip chart. Try to come to a group consensus on each item.

Setting SMART Goals

Goal setting is critical to effective time management strategies. It is the single most important life skill that, unfortunately, most people never learn how to do properly. Goal setting can be used in every single area of your life, including financial, physical, personal development, relationships, or even spiritual. According to Brian Tracy's book Goals, fewer than 3% of people have clear, written goals, and a plan for getting there. Setting goals puts you ahead of the pack!

Some people blame everything that goes wrong in their life on something or someone else. They take the role of a victim and they give all their power and control away. Successful people instead dedicate themselves towards taking responsibility for their lives, no matter what the unforeseen or uncontrollable events. Live in the present: the past cannot be changed, and the future is the direct result of what you do right now!

The Three P's

Setting meaningful, long-term goals is a giant step toward achieving your dreams. In turn, setting and achieving short-term goals can help you accomplish the tasks you'll need to achieve the long-term ones. It is also important to make sure that all of your goals unleash the power of the three P's:

POSITIVE: Who could get fired up about a goal such as "Find a career that's not boring"? Goals should be phrased positively, so they help you feel good about yourself and what you're trying to accomplish. A better alternative might be this: "Enroll in pre-law classes so I can help people with legal problems someday."

PERSONAL: Goals must be personal. They must reflect your own dreams and values, not those of friends, family, or the media. When crafting your goal statement, always use the word "I" in the sentence to brand it as your own. When your goals are personal, you'll be more motivated to succeed and take greater pride in your accomplishments.

POSSIBLE: When setting goals, be sure to consider what's possible and within your control. Getting into an Ivy League university may be possible if you are earning good grades but unrealistic if you're struggling. In the latter case, a more reasonable goal might be to attend a university or trade school that offers courses related to your chosen career. You might also pursue volunteer work that would strengthen your college applications.

The SMART Way

SMART is a convenient acronym for the set of criteria that a goal must have in order for it to be realized by the goal achiever.

Specific: Success coach Jack Canfield states in his book <u>The Success Principles</u> that, "Vague goals produce vague results." In order for you to achieve a goal, you must be very clear about what exactly you want. Often creating a list of benefits that the accomplishment of your goal will bring to your life, will give your mind a compelling reason to pursue that goal.

Measurable: It's crucial for goal achievement that you are able to track your progress towards your goal. That's why all goals need some form of objective measuring system so that you can stay on track and become motivated when you enjoy the sweet taste of quantifiable progress.

Achievable: Setting big goals is great, but setting unrealistic goals will just de-motivate you. A good goal is one that challenges, but is not so unrealistic that you have virtually no chance of accomplishing it.

Relevant: Before you even set goals, it's a good idea to sit down and define your core values and your life purpose because it's these tools which ultimately decide how and what goals you choose for your life. Goals, in and of themselves, do not provide any happiness. Goals that are in harmony with our life purpose do have the power to make us happy.

Timed: Without setting deadlines for your goals, you have no real compelling reason or motivation to start working on them. By setting a deadline, your subconscious mind begins to work on that goal, night and day, to bring you closer to achievement.

Prioritizing Your Goals

Achieving challenging goals requires a lot of mental energy. Instead of spreading yourself thin by focusing on several goals at once, invest your mental focus on one goal, the most important goal right now. When you are prioritizing, choose a goal that will have the greatest impact on your life compared to how long it will take to achieve. A large part of goal setting is not just identifying what you want, but also identifying what you must give up in your life in order to get it. Most people are unwilling to make a conscious decision to give up the things in their life necessary to achieve their goals.

Visualization

Emotionalizing and visualizing your goal will help you create the desire to materialize it into your life. One of the best visualization tools is a vision board. Simply find a magazine, cut out pictures that resonate with the goal that you want to achieve, glue them onto a piece of poster board, and place that board somewhere that you can view it several times a day.

In order for visualization to work, it's necessary that you emotionalize your goal as much as possible. Create a list of the benefits you will see when you achieve your goal and concentrate on how that will make you feel.

Chapter 2 – Prioritizing Your Time

Time management is about more than just managing our time; it is about managing ourselves, in relation to time. It is about setting priorities and taking charge. It means changing habits or activities that cause us to waste time. It means being willing to experiment with different methods and ideas to enable you to find the best way to make maximum use of time.

The 80/20 Rule

The 80/20 rule, also known as Pareto's Principle, states that 80% of your results come from only 20% of your actions. Across the board, you will find that the 80/20 principle is pretty much right on with most things in your life. For most people, it really comes down to analyzing what you are spending your time on. Are you focusing in on the 20% of activities that produce 80% of the results in your life?

The Urgent/Important Matrix

Great time management means being effective as well as efficient. Managing time effectively, and achieving the things that you want to achieve, means spending your time on things that are important and not just urgent. To do this, you need to distinguish clearly between what is urgent and what is important:

- **Important**: These are activities that lead to achieving your goals and have the greatest impact on your life.

- **Urgent**: These activities demand immediate attention, but are often associated with someone else's goals rather than our own.

This concept, coined the Eisenhower Principle, is said to be how former US President Dwight Eisenhower organized his tasks. It was rediscovered and brought into the mainstream as the Urgent/Important Matrix by Stephen Covey in his 1994 business classic, The Seven Habits of Highly Effective People. The Urgent/Important Matrix is a powerful way of organizing tasks based on priorities. Using it helps you overcome the natural tendency to focus on urgent activities, so that you can have time to focus on what's truly important.

The Urgent/Important Matrix:

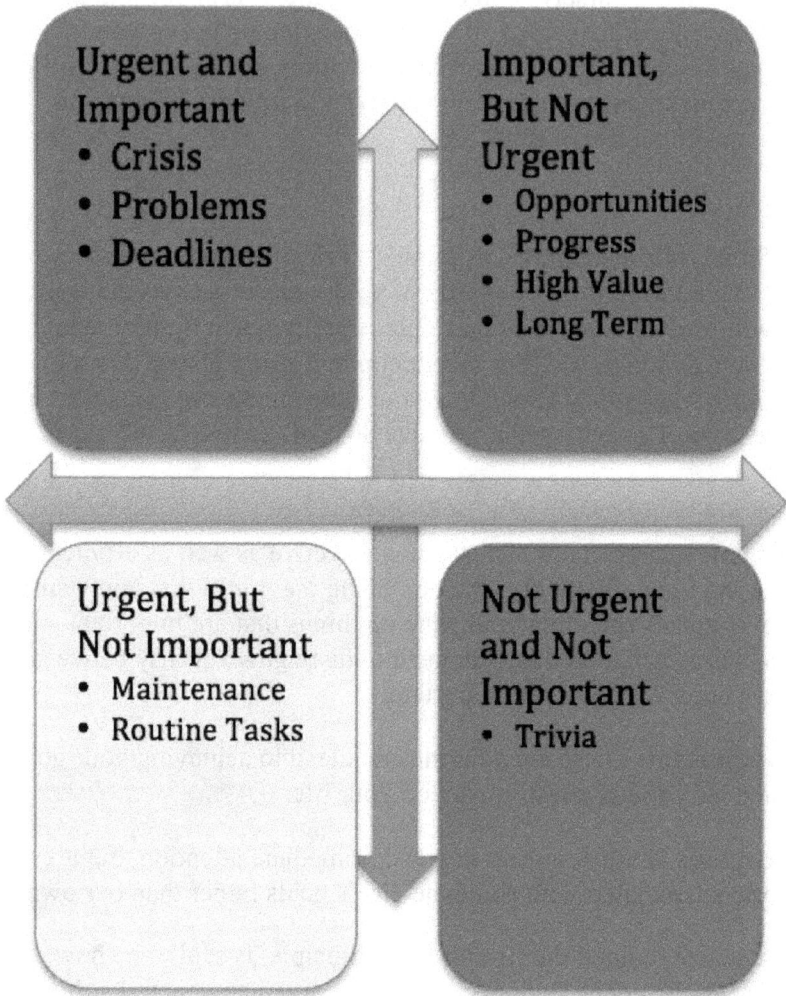

Urgent and Important • Crisis • Problems • Deadlines	Important, But Not Urgent • Opportunities • Progress • High Value • Long Term
Urgent, But Not Important • Maintenance • Routine Tasks	Not Urgent and Not Important • Trivia

- **Urgent And Important**: Activities in this area relate to dealing with critical issues as they arise and meeting significant commitments. *Perform these duties now.*

- **Important, But Not Urgent:** These success-oriented tasks are critical to achieving goals. *Plan to do these tasks next.*

- **Urgent, But Not Important:** These chores do not move you forward toward your own goals. Manage by delaying them, cutting them short, and rejecting requests from others. *Postpone these chores.*

- **Not Urgent And Not Important:** These trivial interruptions are just a distraction, and should be avoided if possible. However, be careful not to mislabel things like time with family and recreational activities as not important. *Avoid these distractions altogether.*

Being Assertive

At times, requests from others may be important and need immediate attention. Often, however, these requests conflict with our values and take time away from working toward your goals. Even if it is something we would like to do but simply don't have the time for, it can be very difficult to say no. One approach in dealing with these types of interruptions is to use a Positive No, which comes in several forms.

- Say no, followed by an honest explanation, such as, "I am uncomfortable doing that because…"

- Say no and then briefly clarify your reasoning without making excuses. This helps the listener to better understand your position. Example: "I can't right now because I have another project that is due by 5 pm today."

- Say no, and then give an alternative. Example: "I don't have time today, but I could schedule it in for tomorrow morning."

- Empathetically repeat the request in your own words, and then say no. Example: "I understand that you need to have this paperwork filed immediately, but I will not be able to file it for you."

- Say yes, give your reasoning for not doing it, and provide an alternative solution. Example: "Yes, I would love to help you by filing this paperwork, but I do not have time until tomorrow morning."

- Provide an assertive refusal and repeat it no matter what the person says. This approach may be most appropriate with aggressive or manipulative people and can be an effective strategy to control your emotions. Example: "I understand how you feel, but I will not [or cannot]…" Remember to stay focused and not become sidetracked into responding to other issues.

Chapter 3 – Planning Wisely

The hallmark of successful time management is being consistently productive each day. Many people use a daily plan to motivate themselves. Having a daily plan and committing to it can help you stay focused on the priorities of that particular day. As well, you are more likely to get things accomplished if you write down your plans for the day.

Creating Your Productivity Journal

Essentially, planning is nothing more than taking a piece of paper and a pen and writing down the tasks and associated steps that you need to take throughout the day to ensure that your goal is completed.

To start, get yourself a spiral notebook and label it as your Personal Productivity Journal or your Professional Productivity Journal. (We recommend keeping a separate journal for work and for your personal life, so you can focus on them at separate times, thus maintaining your optimal work/life balance.) Label each page with the day and the date and what needs to be done that particular day. Next, prioritize each task in order of importance. Highlight the top three items and focus on those first. Cross off items as you complete them. Items that are not completed should be carried over to the next page.

Maximizing the Power of Your Productivity Journal

Personal development expert Brian Tracy believes that when you write down your action list the night before, your subconscious mind focuses on that plan while you sleep. By planning the night before, you will also start fresh and focused on the most important tasks for the day. Of course, you will want to review your list in the morning, but you will have a head start on your day.

Always have your productivity journal with you during the day to avoid becoming sidetracked. Crossing off completed tasks will give your subconscious mind a tremendous amount of satisfaction. This will also help to maintain your motivation to complete the remaining items on your action list.

If you find yourself moving uncompleted tasks over into the following day, and the day after that, then you need to ask yourself why that task is on your list in the first place and what value it has in your life. If you postpone a task three times, it does not belong on your action list.

The Glass Jar: Rocks, Pebbles, Sand, and Water

There is a story about time management that uses a glass jar, rocks, stones, pebbles, sand, and water to illustrate how to plan your day. The glass jar represents the time you have each day, and each item that goes into it represents an activity with a priority relative to its size.

Rocks: The general idea is to fill your glass jar first with rocks. Plan each day around your most important tasks that will propel you toward achieving your goals. These represent your highest priority projects and deadlines with the greatest value, often *important, but not urgent* tasks that move you toward your goals.

Pebbles: Next, fill in the space between the rocks with pebbles. These represent tasks that are *urgent, and important*, but contribute less to important goals. Without proper planning, these tasks are often unexpected, and left unmanaged, can quickly fill your day. Working to reduce these tasks will give you more time to work toward your goals.

Sand: Now add sand to fill your jar. In other words, schedule *urgent, but not important* tasks, only after important tasks. These activities are usually routine or maintenance tasks that do not directly contribute to your goals.

Water: Finally, pour water into your jar. These trivial time-wasters are neither important nor urgent and take you away from working toward high return activities and your goals.

If you commit to this approach to planning your days, you will see as time goes on that you are able to achieve more in less time. Instead of finishing things in a mad rush to meet deadlines, each day will be organized and become more productive and profitable. You will also notice yourself spending less time on activities that are of little to no value. And because you have a clear vision for dealing with competing priorities, the level of stress in your life will diminish, which will allow you to become even more focused and productive.

Chunk, Block, and Tackle

Large projects can sometimes be so overwhelming it is difficult to even plan to start them. This time management technique is ideal for taking on these jobs. Simply break down the project into manageable chunks, block off time to work on the project, and then tackle it with a single-minded focus.

- **Chunk**: Break large projects into specific tasks that can be completed in less than 15 minutes.

- **Block:** Rather than scheduling the entire project all at once, block out set times to complete specific chunks as early in the day as possible. This should allow you to ignore most interruptions and focus on just this task.

- **Tackle**: Now tackle the specific task, focusing only on this task rather than the project as a whole. Once completed, you will feel a sense of accomplishment from making progress on the project.

Ready, Fire, Aim!

We've all heard the saying, "Ready, Aim, Fire!" Often in time management planning, it is better to think "Ready, Fire, Aim!" instead. This is because most people aim for the target, and then they keep aiming at the target, but they never seem to fire. They get so caught up with the planning that they fail to take action. This is just another form of procrastination, which we will discuss in a moment. Better to take a shot and see how close you were to the target.

- **Ready**! Do not over-plan each of your actions. By the time you fire, the target may have moved.

- **Fire**! Remember the 80/20 rule and just take action. Even if you don't hit the bull's eye, you'll probably still hit the target.

- **Aim**! Make new plans based on new information. Readjust your aim based on where you hit the target.

Chapter 4 – Tackling Procrastination

Procrastination means delaying a task (or even several tasks) that should be a priority. The ability to overcome procrastination and tackle the important actions that have the biggest positive impact in your life is a hallmark of the most successful people out there.

Why We Procrastinate

There are many reasons why we tend to procrastinate, including:

- No clear deadline

- Inadequate resources available (time, money, information, etc.)

- Don't know where to begin

- Task feels overwhelming

- No passion for doing the work

- Fear of failure or success

Nine Ways to Overcome Procrastination

Your ability to select your most important task at any given moment, and then to start on that task and get it done both quickly and well, will probably have greatest impact on your success than any other quality or skill you can develop! If you nurture the habit of setting clear priorities and getting important tasks quickly finished, the majority of your time management issues will simply fade away.

Here are some ways to get moving on those tough tasks.

- **Delete it**. What are the consequences of not doing the task at all? Consider the 80/20 rule; maybe it doesn't need to be done in the first place.

- **Delegate**. If the task is important, ask yourself if it's really something that you are responsible for doing in the first place. Know your job description and ask if the task is part of your responsibilities. Can the task be given to someone else?

- **Do it now**. Postponing an important task that needs to be done only creates feelings of anxiety and stress. Do it as early in the day as you can.

Ask for advice. Asking for help from a trusted mentor, supervisor, coach, or expert can give you some great insight on where to start and the steps for completing a project.

CHOP IT UP. Break large projects into milestones, and then into actionable steps. As Bob Proctor says, "Break it down into the ridiculous." Huge things don't look as big when you break it down as small as you can.

- **Obey the 15 minute rule**. To reduce the temptation of procrastination, each actionable step on a project should take no more than 15 minutes to complete.

- **Have clear deadlines**. Assign yourself a deadline for projects and milestones and write it down in your day planner or calendar. Make your deadlines known to other people who will hold you accountable.

- **Give yourself a reward**. Celebrate the completion of project milestones and reward yourself for getting projects done on time. It will provide positive reinforcement and motivate you toward your goals.

- **Remove distractions**. You need to establish a positive working environment that is conducive to getting your work done. Remove any distractions.

Eat That Frog!

"If the first thing you do each morning is to eat a live frog, you can go through the day with the satisfaction of knowing that that is probably the worst thing that is going to happen to you all day long!"

Your frog is the task that will have the greatest impact on achieving your goals, and the task that you are most likely to procrastinate starting.

Another version of this saying is, "If you have to eat two frogs, eat the ugliest one first!"

This is another way of saying that if you have two important tasks before you, start with the biggest, hardest, and most important task first. Discipline yourself to begin immediately and then to persist until the task is complete before you go on to something else. You must resist the temptation to start with the easier task. You must also continually remind yourself that one of the most important decisions you make each day is your choice of what you will do immediately and what you will do later, or postpone indefinitely.

Finally, "If you have to eat a live frog, it does not pay to sit and look at it for a very long time!"

The key to reaching high levels of performance and productivity is for you to develop the lifelong habit of tackling your major task first thing each morning. Don't spend excessive time planning what you will do. You must develop the routine of "eating your frog" before you do anything else and without taking too much time to think about it.

Successful, effective people are those who launch directly into their major tasks and then discipline themselves to work steadily and single-mindedly until those tasks are complete.

In the business world, you are paid and promoted for achieving specific, measurable results. You are paid for making a valuable contribution that is expected of you. But many employees confuse activity with accomplishment and this causes one of the biggest problems in organizations today, which is failure to execute.

Chapter 5 – Crisis Management

With better planning, improved efficiency, and increased productivity, the number of crises you encounter should decline. However, you can't plan for everything, so in this module we'll look at what to do when a crisis does occur.

When the Storm Hits

The key to successfully handling a crisis is to move quickly and decisively, but carefully.

The first thing to do when a crisis hits is to identify the point of contact and make them aware of the situation. (For this module, we'll assume that point of contact is you.)

Then, you will want to gather and analyze the data.

- What happened?

- What were the direct causes? What were the indirect causes?

- What will happen next? What could happen next?

- What events will this impact?

- Who else needs to know about this?

Above all, take the time to do thorough, proper research. You don't want to jump into action based on erroneous information and make the crisis worse.

You will also want to identify the threshold time: the time that you have before the situation moves out of your control, or becomes exponentially worse. You may also find that the crisis will resolve itself after a certain point of time.

Creating a Plan

Once you have gathered the data, it's time to create a plan. The best approach is to identify the problem, decide on a solution, break it down into parts, and create a timeline.

Below is a sample Action Plan for Quarter One Status Report.

Executing the Plan

As you execute the plan, make sure that you continue evaluating if the plan is working. In the example we just looked at, perhaps after gathering project information, you realize you need more details on a particular item. It would then be appropriate to add that step and make sure you are still on track to meet your timeline.

During execution, it is important to stay organized and on top of events to make sure that your plan is still applicable. This will also help you deliver accurate, effective communication to others affected by the crisis. (In this example, your manager is probably pretty anxious to get that report!)

Lessons Learned

After the crisis is over, take a moment to look at why it happened and how to prevent it in the future. In the example we used, our Quarter One Status Report was not completed on time. (In fact, it sounds like we forgot to start it altogether!) The planning and prioritizing tools that we are discussing in this workshop should help prevent those kinds of emergencies. However, you will likely find that you're always adjusting and perfecting your approach, so it is important to learn from the times where those tools don't work.

You can even be prepared for disasters that can't be predicted, such as illness, fire, or theft. In the case of illness, for example, you could prepare a short contingency plan indicating who will be responsible for your correspondence, projects, and general responsibilities in case you are ill for an extended period. Make sure you share these plans with the appropriate people so that they can be prepared as well.

Chapter 6 – Organizing Your Workspace

In order to effectively manage your time and to be productive each day, you must create an appropriate environment. By eliminating clutter, setting up an effective filing system, gathering essential tools, and managing workflow, you will be well on your way to creating an effective workspace.

De-Clutter

Removing clutter is itself a time-consuming task, but a cluttered workspace significantly impairs your ability to find things, and you will get the time back that you invest – and more! To retrieve materials quickly, you'll need an effective filing system that includes three basic kinds of files:

- **Working files**: Materials used frequently and needed close at hand.

- **Reference files**: Information needed only occasionally.

- **Archival files:** Materials seldom retrieved but that must be kept. For ease of retrieval, organize files in the simplest way possible. For example, you could label files with a one or two word tag and arrange the files alphabetically.

Once clutter has been eliminated and other materials have been filed, the effective workspace includes only what is essential: a set of three trays to control the workflow on your desk (see the next topic), standard office supplies, a computer, and a telephone. Everything else, except for what you are working on at the moment, can and should be filed where it can be retrieved as needed.

Managing Workflow

How do you process the mountain of material that collects in your paper and electronic in-baskets? The answer is one piece of paper, one electronic message at a time. Many time management experts agree that the most effective people act on an item the first time it is touched.

Although difficult at first, the practice can become habitual, and is made easier with the four Ds:

- **DO**: If a task can be completed in two minutes or less, do it immediately.

- **DELETE**: If the material is trash or junk, delete it. Or, if it's something that you might use later on, file it, and move on.

- **DEFER**: If the task is one that can't be completed quickly and is not a high priority item, simply defer it.

- **DELEGATE**: If a task is not yours to do, then delegate it.

Remember, to take the S.T.I.N.G. out of feeling overwhelmed about a task, follow these steps:

- Select one task to do at a time.

- Time yourself using a clock for no more than one hour.

- Ignore everything else during that time.

- No breaks or interruptions should be permitted.

- Give yourself a reward when the time is up.

Dealing with E-mail

Electronic communication can be managed just as easily and as quickly as paper with the four D's that we just discussed. However, there are some other key ideas that will help you maximize your e-mail time.

- Like other routine tasks (such as returning phone calls, handling paper mail, and checking voice mail), e-mail is best handled in batches at regularly scheduled times of the day.

- Ask your e-mail contacts to use specific subject lines, and make sure to use them yourself. This will help you to determine whether your incoming mail is business or personal, urgent or trivial.

- Once you know the subject of the message, open and read urgent e-mails, and respond accordingly. Non-urgent e-mails, like jokes, can be read later. Delete advertising-related e-mail that you have no interest in, or which you consider spam.

- Use your e-mail system to its fullest potential. Create folders for different topics or projects, or by senders. Most e-mail systems also allow you to create folders and add keywords or categories to messages, which makes information retrieval much easier.

- Many e-mail programs allow you to create rules that automatically move messages to the appropriate folder. This can help you follow your e-mail plan.

- Finally, don't forget to delete e-mail from your trash can and junk folder on a regular basis.

Using Calendars

To manage all of the things that you have to do, it's important to organize your reminders into a small number of calendars and lists that can be reviewed regularly. A calendar (paper or electronic) is the obvious place to record meetings, appointments, and due dates.

People with multiple responsibilities, an annual calendar organized by areas of responsibility (e.g., budget, personnel, schedule, planning, and miscellaneous) may be especially valuable. For each of these areas, one can list the major responsibilities month by month and thereby see at a glance what tasks must be completed in a given month of the year.

Don't forget the Productivity Journal that we discussed earlier. This can be a valuable tool for organizing tasks, identifying patterns, improving workflow, and recording work completed.

Chapter 7 – Delegating Made Easy

If you work on your own, there's only so much you can get done, no matter how hard you work. As well, everyone needs help and support, and there is no shame in asking for assistance. One of the most common ways of overcoming this limitation is to learn how to delegate your work to other people. If you do this well, you can quickly build a strong and successful team of people.

At first sight, delegation can feel like more hassle than it's worth. However, by delegating effectively, you can hugely expand the amount of work that you can deliver. When you arrange the workload so that you are working on the tasks that have the highest priority for you, and other people are working on meaningful and challenging assignments, you have a recipe for success.

Remember, to delegate effectively, choose the right tasks to delegate, identify the right people to delegate to, and delegate in the right way. There's a lot to this, but you'll achieve so much more once you're delegating effectively!

When to Delegate

Delegation allows you to make the best use of your time and skills, and it helps other people in the team grow and develop to reach their full potential in the organization. Delegation is a win-win situation for all involved, but only when done correctly. Keep these criteria in mind when deciding if a task should be delegated:

- The task should provide an opportunity for growth of another person's skills.

- Weigh the effort to properly train another person against how often the task will reoccur.

- Delegating certain critical tasks may jeopardize the success of your project.

- Management tasks, such as performance reviews, and tasks specifically assigned to you, should not be delegated.

To Whom Should You Delegate?

Once you have decided to delegate a task, think about the possible candidates for accepting the task. Things to think about include:

- What experience, knowledge, skills, and attitude does the person already have?

- What training or assistance might they need?

- Do you have the time and resources to provide any training needed?

- What is the individual's preferred work style? Do they do well on their own or do they require more support and motivation? How independent are they?

- What does he or she want from his or her job?

- What are his or her long-term goals and interest, and how do these align with the work proposed?

- What is the current workload of this person? Does the person have time to take on more work?

- Will you delegating this task require reshuffling of other responsibilities and workloads?

When you first start to delegate to someone, you may notice that he or she takes longer than you do to complete tasks. This is because you are an expert in the field and the person you have delegated to is still learning. Be patient: if you have chosen the right person to delegate to, and you are delegating correctly, you will find that he or she quickly becomes competent and reliable. Also, try to delegate to the lowest possible organizational level. The people who are closest to the work are best suited for the task because they have the most intimate knowledge of the detail of everyday work. This also increases workplace efficiency, and helps to develop people.

How Should You Delegate?

Delegation doesn't have to be all or nothing. There are several different levels of delegation, each with different levels of delegate independence and delegator supervision.

The Spheres of Independence

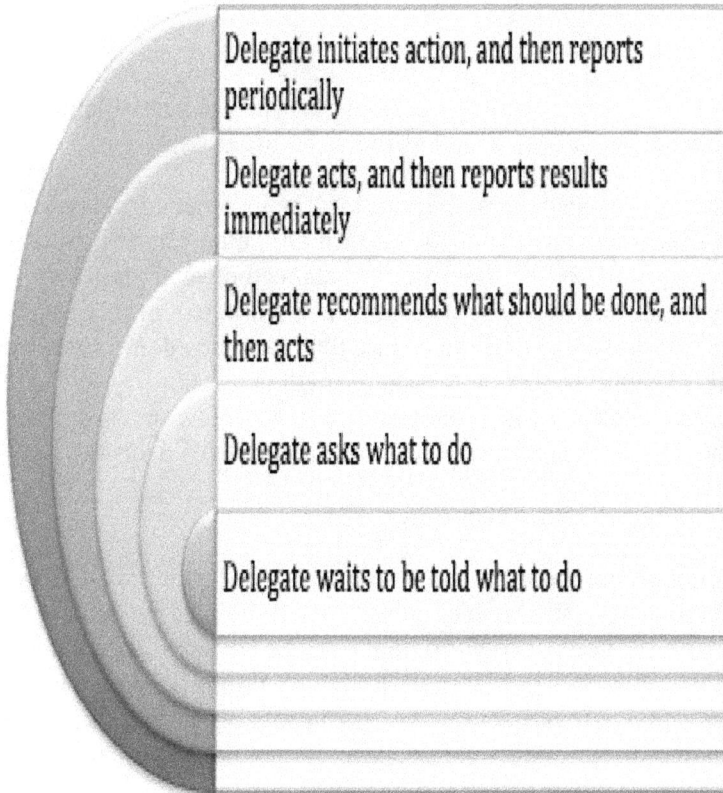

Delegate initiates action, and then reports periodically

Delegate acts, and then reports results immediately

Delegate recommends what should be done, and then acts

Delegate asks what to do

Delegate waits to be told what to do

People often move throughout these spheres during the delegation process. Your goal should be to get the delegate to one of the outer three spheres, depending on the task being performed. Make sure you match the amount of responsibility with the amount of authority. Understand that you can delegate some responsibility, but you can't delegate away ultimate accountability. The buck stops with you!

Keeping Control

Now, once you have worked through the above steps, make sure you brief your team member appropriately. Take time to explain why they were chosen for the job, what's expected from them during the project, the goals you have for the project, all timelines and deadlines, and the resources on which they can draw. Work together to develop a schedule for progress updates, milestones, and other key project points.

You will want to make sure that the team member knows that you want to know if any problems occur, and that you are available for any questions or guidance needed as the work progresses.

We all know that as managers, we shouldn't micro-manage. However, this doesn't mean we must abdicate control altogether. In delegating effectively, we have to find the difficult balance between giving enough space for people to use their abilities, while still monitoring and supporting closely enough to ensure that the job is done correctly and effectively. One way to encourage growth is to ask for recommended solutions when delegates come to you with a problem, and then help them explore those solutions and reach a decision.

The Importance of Full Acceptance

Set aside enough time to thoroughly review any delegated work that was delivered to you. If possible, only accept good quality, fully complete work. If you accept work that you are not satisfied with, your team member does not learn to do the job properly. Worse than this, you accept a new project that you will probably need to complete yourself. Not only does this overload you, it means that you don't have the time to do your own job properly.

Of course, when good work is returned to you, make sure to both recognize and reward the effort. As a leader, you should get in the practice of complimenting members of your team every time you are impressed by what they have done. This effort on your part will go a long way toward building team members' self-confidence and efficiency now and in the future.

Chapter 8 – Setting a Ritual

For most people, the word "ritual" typically conjures up an image of a boring, repetitive life, with every moment controlled and managed, and no room for spontaneity. Rituals and routines, however, can actually help increase the spontaneity and fun in your life. Because routine tasks are already planned for, you have more energy to spend on the tasks that will bring you closer to your goals and bring more joy to your life.

What is a Ritual?

The Random House Dictionary defines a ritual as, "any practice or pattern of behavior regularly performed in a set manner."

In fact, you can build any type of ritual in three easy steps.

- **Identify the Task.** Let's say you want to build an exercise ritual.

- **Identify the Time and/or Trigger.** For example, perhaps you normally exercise right after work.

- **Identify the Sub-Tasks.** For you, perhaps your ritual involves going to the gym, getting changed, stretching, doing 45 minutes on the treadmill, performing three reps of weights, and doing a lap around the pool to finish things off. Then, you shower and go home.

Remember, a ritual shouldn't be set in stone. Once you establish a ritual, it can be modified at any point in time, depending on what works for you. With our exercise example, you could easily decide to exercise before work or even at lunch and still use the basic task and sub-tasks.

Ritualizing Sleep, Meals, and Exercise

These three items are essential to ritualize. Here are some ideas.

- **Sleep:** Establish a ritual for half an hour before you sleep. This might include filling out your Productivity Journal for the next day, enjoying a cup of tea, taking a warm bath, and/or performing some stretches. All of these activities will help you wind down and sleep better. It is best to try to go to bed at around the same time every night, too.

- **Meals:** Take a half hour each weekend to plan meals for the next week, including lunches and suppers. Then, make a grocery list and get everything you will need. Appliances like slow cookers and delayed-start ovens can also help you make sure supper is ready when you are.

- **Exercise:** Try to exercise for one hour three times a week, or half an hour each day. One easy way is to go for a brisk walk at lunch, or do yoga in the morning before work.

Example Rituals

Here are some rituals that many people find helpful in maximizing their time:

- Instead of checking e-mail, news, and Web sites throughout the day, set aside one or several periods (for example, morning, noon, and at the end of the day). Then, batch and sequence your activities (for example, e-mail, news, and Facebook). You can batch many types of tasks in this way for maximum efficiency.

- Set up a system for maintaining your Productivity Journal. This can be as simple as ten minutes in the morning to update the day's list, ten minutes at noon to update what you have done already, and ten minutes at day's end to evaluate today and create a starting list for tomorrow.

- In the morning, perform your tasks in an organized, routine manner. You can also lay out your clothes and prepare your lunch the night before for maximum efficiency.

Using Rituals to Maximize Time

Once you have been using a ritual for a while, you may find that you have bits of extra time here and there. For example, you may find that by establishing an exercise ritual, you finish five or ten minutes earlier because you know exactly what you're going to do at the gym. At the end of the day, you may find that you have a half hour or more of unexpected time.

This is where the "Trigger" part of rituals can come into play. Instead of setting a specific time of day, you choose a situation or an event that will cause a ritual to come into play.

Some examples:

- During a break at work or at home, read for ten minutes.

- Take one minute to do some deep breathing and stretches.

- Take five minutes to clean off your desk or some other small area.

- Take ten minutes to update your Personal Productivity Journal.

- Set aside one lunch hour a week to do personal errands. Or, make a list at the beginning of each week, and do one a day.

Chapter 9 – Meeting Management

Meetings are often seen as a necessary evil of office life. Few people look forward to meetings, and with good reason. Too many meetings lack purpose and structure. However, with just a few tools, you can make any meeting a much better use of everyone's time.

Deciding if a Meeting is Necessary

The first thing you need to decide is if a formal meeting is necessary. Perhaps those morning staff meetings could be reduced to a few times a week instead of every day, or maybe they could take place over morning coffee and be more informal. (In the next module, we'll talk about some alternatives to meetings, too.)

If a formal meeting is necessary, divide your attendees into two groups: participants and observers. Let people know what group they belong in so that they can decide whether they want to attend. If you send out a report after the meeting, that may be enough for some people.

Using the PAT Approach

We use the PAT approach to prepare for and schedule meetings.

- **Purpose:** What is the purpose of the meeting? We usually state this in one short sentence. Example: "This meeting is to review the new invoice signing policy." This helps people evaluate if they need to be there. It will also help you build the agenda and determine if the meeting was successful.

- **Agenda:** This is the backbone of the meeting. It should be created well in advance of the meeting, sent to all participants and observers, and be used during the meeting to keep things on track.

- **Time frame:** How long will the meeting be? Typically, meetings should not exceed one hour. (In fact, we recommend a fifty minute meeting, starting at five past the hour and ending five minutes before the hour.) If the meeting needs to be longer, make sure you include breaks, or divide it into two or more sessions.

Building the Agenda

Before the meeting, make a list of what needs to be discussed, how long you believe it will take, and the person who will be presenting the item. Here is an example.

Once the agenda is complete, send it to all participants and observers, preferably with the meeting request, and preferably two to three days before the meeting. Make sure you ask for everyone's approval, including additions or deletions. If you do make changes, send out a single updated copy 24 hours before the meeting.

Keeping Things on Track

Before the meeting, post the agenda on a flip chart, whiteboard, or PowerPoint slide. Spend the first five minutes of the meeting going over the agenda and getting approval. During the meeting, take minutes with the agenda as a framework.

(Although this informal structure will be sufficient for most meetings, more formal meetings may require more formal minutes.)

Your job as chairperson is to keep the meeting running according to the agenda. If an item runs past its scheduled time, ask the group if they think more time is needed to discuss the item. If so, how do they want to handle it? They can reduce the time for other items, remove other items altogether, schedule an offline follow-up session, or schedule another meeting. No matter what the group agrees to, make sure that they stick to their decision.

At the end of the meeting, get agreement that all items on the agenda were sufficiently covered. This will identify any gaps that may require follow-up and it will give people a positive sense of accomplishment about the meeting.

Making Sure the Meeting Was Worthwhile

After the meeting, send out a summary of the meeting, including action items, to all participants and observers, and anyone else who requires a copy. Action items should be clearly indicated, with start and end dates, and progress dates if applicable. If follow-up meetings were scheduled, these should also be communicated.

Chapter 10 – Alternatives to Meetings

Sometimes, a face-to-face meeting isn't the best solution. In this module, we will explore alternatives to meetings that can help you and your team save time and be more productive.

Don't forget that even if you use a meeting alternative, you should still use the PAT approach that we discussed in the last module, take minutes, and distribute post-meeting notes and action items.

Instant Messaging and Chat Rooms

Instant message applications and chat rooms can be a great alternative to meetings, especially if meeting members are separated by distance.

Some things to remember:

- Make sure you have an agenda and stick to it.

- The chairperson's role in keeping things on track is more important than ever.

- Set some ground rules at the beginning of the meeting to eliminate distractions such as emoticons, sounds, and acronyms.

- Make sure you keep a record of the meeting.

Some applications to try:

- Campfire

- Meeting Pal

- Microsoft Office Communicator

- Windows Live Messenger

Teleconferencing

If more personal contact and real-time sharing is needed, try a teleconferencing system like Adobe's Acrobat.com, Microsoft Live Meeting, or Citrix's GoToMeeting.

Most teleconferencing applications feature:

- Screen sharing

- Collaboration tools

- Interactive whiteboards

- Voice and text chat support

- Meeting recording capabilities (which can serve as minutes)

Again, remember the PAT approach, and remember to keep minutes and action lists.

E-Mail Lists and Online Groups

If your meeting group requires ongoing, interactive communication, rather than periodic face-to-face gatherings, an e-mail list, forum, or online group can be an effective tool.

There are a few options for these online tools. If your organization has the infrastructure in place, you may be able to set up something on site. If your organization doesn't have such an infrastructure, there are many free tools out there, including Google Groups, Yahoo Groups, and Convos.

A few things to keep in mind if you are going to use this sort of solution:

- Having a moderator is essential. These types of tools can quickly get out of control without proper supervision. You'll want to make sure members stay on topic and stay professional.

- Make sure you monitor the time spent on these tools. Setting a daily or weekly update or delivery time might be a good idea.

- Just like a meeting, an online list or group should have a purpose and stick to it.

Collaboration Applications

A more sophisticated electronic tool that can reduce the need for meetings is collaboration applications. Systems like Microsoft

SharePoint, Wrike, Pelotonics, Google Docs, and Basecamp can give users interaction and collaboration tools from any location.

These sorts of tools may be most beneficial for project meetings, or situations where users need to peer review each other's work.

Once again, these tools must have their purpose clearly stated, and participants must make sure that these time-saving tools don't turn into time wasters.

Additional Titles

The 90 Minute Guide series of books covers a variety of general business skills and are intended to be completed in 90 minutes or less. It is an effective way for building your skill set and can be used to acquire professional development units needed by project managers and other industries to maintain their certification. For the availability of titles please see

https://www.silvercitypublications.com/shop/.

No. 1 - Appreciative Inquiry

No. 2 - Assertiveness and Self Control

No. 3 - Attention Management

No. 4 - Body Language Basics

No. 5 - Business Acumen

No. 6 - Business and Etiquette

No. 7 - Change Management

No. 8 - Coaching and Mentoring

No. 9 - Communications Strategies

No. 10 - Conflict Resolution

No. 11 - Creative Problem Solving

No. 12 - Delivering Constructive Criticism

No. 13 - Developing Creativity

No. 14 - Developing Emotional Intelligence

No. 15 - Developing Interpersonal Skills

No. 16 - Developing Social Intelligence

No. 17 - Employee Motivation

No. 18 - Facilitation Skills

No. 19 - Goal Setting and Getting Things Done

No. 20 - Knowledge Management Fundamentals

No. 21 - Leadership and Influence

No. 22 - Lean Process and Six Sigma Basics

No. 23 - Managing Anger

No. 24 - Meeting Management

No. 25 - Negotiation Skills

No. 26 - Networking Inside a Company

No. 27 - Networking Outside a Company

No. 28 - Office Politics for Managers

No. 29 - Organizational Skills

No. 30 - Performance Management

No. 31 - Presentation Skills

No. 32 - Public Speaking

No. 33 - Servant Leadership